Pathways of Song

(REVISED EDITION)

COMPILED, ARRANGED
TRANSLATED, EDITED

by

FRANK LaFORGE

and

WILL EARHART

VOLUME ONE, TWO, THREE, FOUR
HIGH VOICE
LOW VOICE

FOREWORD

The purpose of this book is to place within reach of students in high schools, as well as those in studios and in schools specializing in music, songs of the greatest beauty, selected from wide fields of classical and folksong literature. Great care has been taken to include only songs that in the main lie in a restricted compass and that, while they are worthy of the attention of the greatest artist and may well find place on the most deserving programs, yet do not require elaborate technique for their effective performance. Musical worth and technical difficulty are thus regarded as not necessarily proportional; and. while musical worth must be maintained at every stage, if study is to develop fine taste and sound musical culture, vocal difficulties may be, and for a time must be, avoided.

Nor does modest vocal proficiency in a student necessarily imply a correspondingly low development of artistic taste. There is no reason why easy songs should be also trivial. On the contrary, good song material is likely to prove as favorable for the development of good vocal technique as it is for the development of good musical taste. The reason is that songs written by the masters, or preserved through long years (whatever their origin) because of their golden worth, are likely, in addition to their other graces, to possess true vocal style. Thus they will be found to lie on the voice, and to prefigure only the forms of a correct vocal technique; while flimsy and illy written music. not only for voice, but also for piano, violin, or any other medium, is likely to disclose ignorance, on the part of the composer, of the proper technical procedures, or else an inability on his part to conceive music in the terms of the particular medium for which he was writing. And the consequence is that such music tends to induce rough and faulty forms of technical action on the part of the young performer essaying it.

Extreme care has been given to the translations. Effort was directed toward making them adhere closely to the original texts, both in general import and in subtleties of mood; and in the case of specific words of distinctive hue or of climacteric force, occurring here and there, English words of like color or force were sought. Euphony and vocal ease were also considered in the choice of words.

In addition to the aims mentioned the editors have sought to include in the books a goodly number of comparatively unhackneyed songs, that appear to have been left to one side, quite undeservedly, by the winds of current interest. It is their hope that in this, as in their other aims, they have met with some degree of success, and have thereby promoted to some extent their cherished purpose, which is to improve and enrich the literature available to students who follow the pleasant *Pathways of Song*.

Frank LaForge

The name of Frank LaForge first came into world prominence as accompanist and piano soloist with Mme. Marcella Sembrich, which position he occupied for ten years. Since then he has rightfully come to be recognized as one of America's foremost accompanists and voice teachers.

Mr. LaForge's grasp of the great songs of the world is comprehensive and profound. Some conception of his knowledge of song literature may be gleaned from the fact that he has a repertoire of over five thousand memorized accompaniments embracing all schools. He has been associated as accompanist and pianist with the outstanding singers of his day, among whom may be mentioned, besides Mme. Sembrich, Mmes. Schumann-Heink, Matzenauer and Lily Pons. Among his voice pupils have been such representative American singers as Marian Anderson, Marie Powers, Lawrence Tibbett, Richard Crooks and many other operatic and concert stars.

It may be safely said that in all probability no living person knows more accurately or has studied more sympathetically the needs of the singer and particularly of the vocal student. The solutions that great artists have brought to bear upon their own problems of interpretation and vocal technique have been observed and weighed by Mr. LaForge in his New York Studio, a studio that may well be called in the true scientific use of the word, a voice laboratory.

It is upon these years of experience in studying the needs of the student singer, particularly as applied to songs that have technical as well as program value, that Mr. LaForge has drawn in compiling these books.

Will Earhart

A truly representative figure in music education, Dr. Will Earhart has been identified with every phase of music in the public schools, an unwavering influence for the elevation of musical standards and the improvement of pedagogic practices.

In addition to his work in the public schools, Dr. Earhart has been a faculty member or superintendent of innumerable summer music schools including those of Northwestern University, Columbia University, Pennsylvania State College, the University of California and Syracuse University. For many years he has been identified with the music department of Carnegie Institute of Technology.

As writer and editor he has a catalog of such length as to preclude listing here, appearing under the imprint of representative American publishers. Specific mention, however, should be made of his *The Eloquent Baton* (a manual for conductors) and *Music to the Listening Ear*, a book for students of music appreciation. He has made many surveys and reports for the United States Bureau of Education. His contributions to musical and educational journals have been enlightening commentaries upon the history, theory, practice and social significance of music education.

He is a past president of the Music Supervisors National Conference and has been active on many committees of that organization. His services are frequently called upon as adjudicator of choral, instrumental and vocal contests.

Dr. Earhart was for many years Director of Public School Music in the city of Pittsburgh.

AIDS IN PROGRAM BUILDING

In order to facilitate the arrangement of programs, the undersigned has selected groups of titles from the four volumes of PATHWAYS OF SONG with contrast of movement and of mood, but with due regard to the period and nationality of the composers. The extra numbers indicated in italics could be substituted, added or used as encores at the discretion of the singer.

With this nucleus other numbers may be added at will. The songs and arias by Handel could be used separately or combined as the singer desires. The groups of folksongs are very colorful and admit of various other arrangements as well as those suggested here.

Frank LaForge

CONTENTS

Calm At Sea
Meeresstille

In 1815, the year in which *Meeresstille* was written, Schubert composed one hundred and forty-six songs, an incredible amount of other music, and taught regularly in his father's school. He was then in his nineteenth year.

In singing *Calm at Sea* the voice should be as motionless, as free from tremulous disquiet, as the sea itself. The vocalist's habit of making the initial moment of a tone stronger than the portion that succeeds it must be avoided. The pattern may be ══════, or slightly ◁══ or ══▷, but not ▷══.

W. von GOETHE
English version by
WILL EARHART

FRANZ SCHUBERT, Op. 3, No. 2

Deep-est still-ness on the wa-ter, Sleeps the sea in calm__ pro-found,
Tie - fe Stil - le herrscht im Was-ser, oh - ne Re-gung ruht__ das Meer,

And the sail - or sees,__ de-ject-ed, Glass-y flat-ness all a - round.
und be-küm-mert sieht__ der Schif-fer glat - te Flä - che rings um - her.

Not a breeze from an - y heav-en; Qui - et as of fear-some
Kei - ne Luft von kei - ner Sei - te! To - des-stil - le fürch-ter-

grave. In the vast un-bro-ken dis-tance Not a rip-ple moves the wave.
lich! In der un-ge-heu-ern Wei-te re - get kei - ne Wel - le sich.

M.W.& Sons 19438-56 Original key

To Friendship
An die Freundschaft

The poetic fervor and individual dramatic character with which Schubert invested every song he wrote drew preference away, for a time, from the less vivid pages of Haydn and Mozart. Now that Schubert's and still later veins of expression have become familiar to us, our taste is rightly expanding to include many kinds of excellence. In this song we should be prepared to accept classical restraint in place of emotional release, and beauty of tone and dignity of phrasing in place of strong dramatic delineation. For establishing good vocal foundations such exchange of values may prove to be advantageous.

English version by
WILL EARHART

JOSEPH HAYDN

Original key - G

M.W.& Sons 19438-56

Serenade

Liebes Mädchen, hör' mir zu

Mr. Henry T. Finck says of this song: *"Liebes Mädchen, hör' mir zu* is as graceful and pretty as a folksong, somewhat suggestive of Schubert's *Heidenröslein."* More praise might well be given it, for the balances of melodic undulation and rhythmic movement are flawless. While the good humor of the song is infectious it is sensitive humor, never transgressing the bounds of good taste.

English translation by
WILL EARHART

JOSEPH HAYDN

Original key - D
M.W. & Sons 19438-56

Though the heav - y clois - ter wall
Then, O love - ly pen - i - tent,
Hal - ten Klo - ster - mau - ern dich
Dann, du schö - ne Dul - de - rin,

May with rig - or bind thee,
Bend thee down, I pray thee,
noch so streng ge - bun - den,
neig' dich zu mir nie - der;

Yet my song to
And, de - spite thy
hab - en mei - ne
und trotz Pfaff' und

thee will call, And, re - joic - ing, find thee.
guard's in - tent, For my songs re - pay me.
Lie - der sich doch zu dir ge - fun - den.
Pri - o - rin lohn mir mei - ne Lie - der!

Below In The Valley
Da unten im Tale

The directness and simplicity of the typical folksong are here apparent. In a musing that holds something of the fragrance of tender memories, something of disillusionment that yet harbors no bitterness, a view of life is disclosed and withdrawn. Brahms' power to add strength and richness to the folksongs he loved, without in the slightest impairing their simplicity or otherwise altering their character, is marvelously illustrated by this accompaniment.

JOHANNES BRAHMS

English version by
WILL EARHART

Original key   *As a prelude it would be well to use the interlude from the last half of measure _one_ of the last line on this page.

M.W. & Sons 19438-5

14

3. When__ ten times I tell you I love on-ly
4. The__ love you have giv - en I grate - ful - ly

3. Und__ wenn i dir's zehn - mal sag', dass i di
4. Für die Zeit, wo du g'liebt mi hast, dank i dir

p

you __ And you will not be - lieve me, what more can I
bear, __ And I hope with an - oth - er you bet - ter may

lich, __ und du willst nit ver - ste - hen, muss i halt wei - ter
schön, __ und i wünsch' dass dir's an-ders-wo bes - ser mag

dim.

do?
fare.
gehn.
gehn.

Eileen Aroon

This matchless melody dates back to the early days of Irish minstrelsy, and was perhaps known in the thirteenth century. The modern version of the text reflects faithfully the spirit and intention of the old verses. As with the Scotch version of the song, *Robin Adair,* the song *Eileen Aroon* came to birth under deeply romantic circumstances.

Handel is said to have declared that he would rather have been the composer of this exquisite air than of all the music he had written. Whether or not he made so extreme a statement, the loveliness of the song is sufficient to lend color to the report. At the same time the sincere purity and simplicity of the song make it one that the humblest as well as the greatest may possess.

Text by
GERALD GRIFFIN

Old Irish Air
Accompaniment by
WILL EARHART

mf

poco rit. e dim.

When, like a di - a - dem, Buds blush a - round the stem,
Is it the ten - der tone, Soft as the stringed harp's moan?
What makes his dawn - ing glow Change-less through joy and woe?

mf *poco rit. e dim.*

mf più lento *ten.* *p a piacere* Verse Ending Final Ending

Which is the fair - est gem? Ei - leen A - roon!
Oh, it is truth a - lone, Ei - leen A - roon! roon!
On - ly the con - stant know, Ei - leen A - roon!

ten.

mf più lento *p colla voce* *a tempo cresc.*

4. I know a valley fair,
      Eileen Aroon!
   I knew a cottage there,
      Eileen Aroon!
   Far in that valley's shade,
   I knew a gentle maid,
   Flower of a hazel glade,
      Eileen Aroon!

5. Who in the song so sweet?
      Eileen Aroon!
   Who in the dance so fleet?
      Eileen Aroon!
   Dear were her charms to me,
   Dearer her laughter free,
   Dearest her constancy,
      Eileen Aroon!

6. Were she no longer true,
      Eileen Aroon!
   What should her lover do?
      Eileen Aroon!
   Fly with his broken chain
   Far o'er the sounding main,
   Never to love again,
      Eileen Aroon!

7. Youth must with time decay,
      Eileen Aroon!
   Beauty must fade away,
      Eileen Aroon!
   Castles are sacked in war,
   Chieftains are scattered far,
   Truth is a fixed star,
      Eileen Aroon!

* For variety, the repeat may also be made by playing this as a chord of dotted half notes, omitting the next three notes and returning to measure three, instead of (as indicated) to measure one.

M.W. & Sons 19438-56

Farewell!
Gute Nacht!

"As a rule, my song is of the declamatory order, and becomes cantilena only where the feeling is most concentrated." So Robert Franz wrote of his songs. Even in the lovely melody of this song there is a hint of narrative, if not of declamation, giving rise to a need for clear enunciation of the text, even though the tonal line must flow undisturbed.

Text by
JOSEPH von EICHENDORFF
English version by
WILL EARHART

ROBERT FRANZ, Op. 5, No. 7

On hill and wood-land is fall-ing
Die Höh'n und Wäl-der schon stei-gen

Fad-ing light from the sky a-bove; A
im-mer tie-fer ins A-bend-gold, ein

bird through branch-es is call-ing: May I greet thee now, my
Vög-lein fragt in den Zwei-gen: ob es Lieb-chen grüs-sen

Original key - F

M.W. & Sons 19438-56

love,___ May I greet thee now, my love? O bird - ling, in vain is thy
sollt',___ ob es Lieb - chen grüs - sen sollt'? O Vög - lein, du hast dich be -

plead-ing, No more in the vale doth she dwell;___ To heav-en's high vault be
tro - gen, sie woh-net nicht mehr im Tal,___ schwing' auf dich zum Him-mels-

speed - ing, And a - bove sing thy last fare - well.___
bo - gen, grüss' sie dro - ben zum letz - ten Mal.___

Watchman's Song

Of lines chanted by watchmen for the comfort of drowsy hearers, as the hours of the night were told, none can have held more appropriate character and weightier meaning than these. Whether the melody was original with the reputed composer, or was rather a traditional one set down by him, is unknown. The echoing and chant-like air has here been provided with a new harmonization and accompaniment, that the distinctive and strongly marked character of the song may be better revealed.

Melody by I. HEFFERMAN
Accompaniment by
WILL EARHART

Text traditional

1. Hark! ye neigh-bors, and hear me tell, Ten now strikes on the bel-fry bell! Ten are the ho-ly com-mand-ments giv'n To man be-low,___ from
2. Hark! ye neigh-bors, and hear me tell, One has pealed on the bel-fry bell! One God a-bove, one___ Lord in-deed, Who bears us up___ in
3. Hark! ye neigh-bors, and hear me tell, Two now rings from the bel-fry bell! Two paths be-fore man-kind are___ free; Oh, neigh-bor, choose___ the

My Dear One's Mouth Is Like The Rose

Mein Mädel hat einen Rosenmund

Brahms' extraordinary fondness for folk music was of life-long duration. His seven books of *Deutsche Volkslieder* were issued only three years before his death. In them a sympathetic master-hand brings the natural flowers of folksong to a complete and appropriate maturity. No over-adornment, through elaborate harmonies or ornate accompanimental figures, is permitted to mar, for instance, the frank and straightforward revelation of the song here offered. One questions, indeed, whether in any other place or under any other treatment it ever became so rightly and truly itself as it does here. Use measures 12 and 13 as Prelude.

English version by
WILL EARHART

JOHANNES BRAHMS

Original key - B♭

M. W. & Sons 19438-56

The Mill-Wheel

Das Mühlrad

Even in the field of folk music, this song is outstanding in point of naturalness, and entire freedom from artificial sentiment. Indeed, at first hearing its simple sincerity almost tends to conceal its worth; but the values that have preserved the song for one hundred fifty years will still be found youthful and appealing to those who cultivate a longer acquaintance with it.

English version by
WILL EARHART

German Folksong, 1784
Accompaniment by
WILL EARHART

M.W.& Sons 19438-56

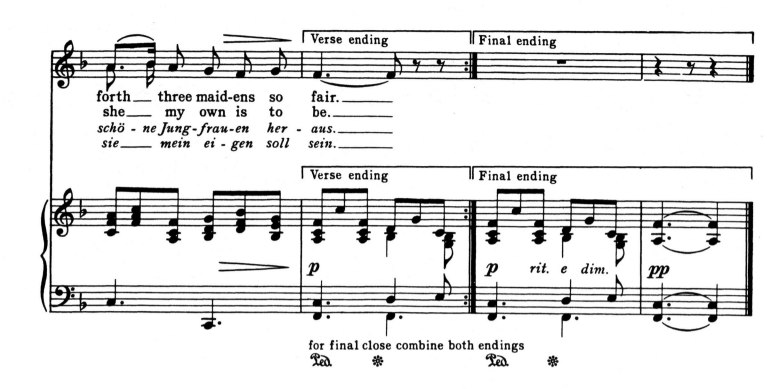

Verse ending | Final ending

forth___ three maid-ens so fair.___
she___ my own is to be.___
schö - ne Jung-frau-en her - aus.___
sie___ mein ei - gen soll sein.___

Verse ending | Final ending

p | *p* *rit. e dim.* *pp*

for final close combine both endings

3. Be - low, in the vale where the mill - wheel turns, The
4. The mill - wheel is bro - ken, but love a - bides, And
5. Oh, part - ing, what tor - ment is part - ing grief! How
3. *Da drun - ten in je - nem Ta - le, Da*
4. *Das Mühl - rad ist___ zer - bro - chen, Die*
5. *Ach, Schei - den, du bit - te - res Schei - den! Wer*

wa - ter flash - es with light;___ Yet___ noth - ing but love does the
e'er when dear ones must part,___ A___ lin - ger - ing clasp of the
came we un - der that chain?___ 'Tis___ part - ing that, laid on my
trei - bet das Was - ser ein Rad,___ Das___ mah - let nichts an - d'res als
Lie - be hat doch kein End;___ Und___ wenn zwei Herz - lieb - chen sich
hat doch das Schei - den er - dacht?___ Das___ hat ja mein jung___ frisch

mill - wheel grind, Tho' turned___ from morn - ing till night.___
hands shall tell The fare - well pray'r of the heart.___
youth - ful heart, Has turned___ my joy in - to pain.___
*Lie - be Von Mor - gen bis A - bend spat.*___
schei - den, So rei - chens ein - an - der die Händ!___
Her - ze Aus Freu - den in Trau - ern ge - bracht.___

* The word *spät* is used here in dialect with no umlaut

M.W.& Sons 19438-56

Lied

The delicate, intangible beauty that is characteristic of Franck hovers over this song. Tragic implications are here, but no poignant outcry shatters the atmospnere of detached, mystic brooding. The artist soul of Franck was ever too suffused with beauty to be wracked by the ugly outlines of present clamoring pain. Feeling that is sincere but sublimated, that is earnest yet restrained, is to be expressed. Avoidance of all artificialities, and concentration upon the musical beauty demanded, will help toward the right interpretation.

LUCIEN PATÉ
English version by
WILL EARHART

CÉSAR FRANCK

Original key - f minor

M.W.& Sons 19438-56

Smiles to the sky._____ And 'neath the bend - ing branch - es_ kneel - ing,
Sou - rit tou - jours._____ Et sous le buis - son qui sur - plom - be,

Where lies my all,_____ A mur - mured voice to me comes steal - ing:
Quand je re - viens,_____ U - ne voix me dit sous la_ tom - be:

"I, too, re - call"._____
"Je me sou - viens"._____

Oh,'Tis The Melody

Thomas Haynes Bayly was, during his brief life, well known in England as poet, dramatist, novelist, and composer. Both words and music to *Gaily the Troubadour* and *The Long Ago* (this latter better known as *Long, Long Ago*) are from his pen, as well as the text alone for *Isle of Beauty,* and many other songs that have long held favor. *Oh, 'Tis The Melody,* in its quiet simplicity, pure and unimpassioned sentiment, and singable quality, is typical of his work.

T. H. BAYLY

Andante, con espressione *(Gently, with expression)*

1. Oh, 'tis the mel - o - dy We heard in form - er years;
2. Aye, I re - mem - ber well Where last I heard that lay!
3. Aye, I re - mem - ber too Who sweet-ly sang and play'd;

Each note re - calls to me For - got - ten smiles and tears:
'Twas in a sun - ny dell, Just at the close of day;
Yet half a - sham'd to view The cir - cle she had made:

Original key - A

M.W.& Sons 19438-56

Dedication
Widmung

A song by Franz may be regarded almost as a translation of a given poem, but with tones substituted for words as the medium of communication. Such substitution took place in the mind of Franz almost unconsciously. Purely musical grace he then entrusted, it would appear, to his sensitive and delicately wrought accompaniments. A "psychic colorist", as Liszt termed him, Franz thus absorbs a poetic frame of mind and faithfully reproduces it in a dual language of tone and text.

Text by
WOLFGANG MÜLLER
English version by
WILL EARHART

ROBERT FRANZ, Op. 14, No. 1

Andante con moto (*Moderately, with motion*)
Innig (*Con affetto*) *With emotion*

O thank me not for songs I ten - der, Grate - ful, in-
O dan - ke nicht für die - se Lie - der, mir ziemt es,

stead, this heart of mine. Song came from thee;— I can but
dank - bar dir zu sein; Du gabst sie mir,— ich ge - be

give thee the songs that ev - er have been thine.
wie - der, was jetzt und einst und e - wig dein.

Original key - A♭
M.W. & Sons 19438 - 56

By The Light Of The Moon

Au Clair de la Lune

Although now rounding out its third century of existence, this song is perennially fresh and youthful. In part its continued attractiveness may be due to its elusive quality. It hints at fleeting moods but decisively delineates none. Shifting half-lights play upon its characters. Yet, withal, it is sensitive, lovely, and lastingly appealing. Perhaps only in France could it have been written. This theme has been utilized by many French composers among them, Debussy.

Air by LULLY
Accompaniment by
WILL EARHART

English version by
WILL EARHART

1. "O Pier - rot, the friend - ly, By the moon's fair light,
2. "In the moon-light stay thee", Friend-ly Pier - rot said:
1. "Au clair de la lu - ne, Mon a - mi Pier - rot,
2. "Au clair de la lu - ne, Pier-rot ré - pon - dit:

Pray thy pen now lend me, For a word I'd write,
"I've no pen to aid thee; I am in my bed.
Prê - te - moi ta plu - me Pour é - crire un mot
Je n'ai pas de plu - me, Je suis dans mon lit

M.W. & Sons 19438-56

Now my can-dle, dy - ing, Holds no more its flame.
To my neigh-bor take thee; She, I think, is there,
Ma chan-delle est mor - te, Je n'ai plus de feu
Va chez la voi-si - ne, Je crois qu'elle y est;

At thy door I'm cry - ing; Ope, in heav-en's name!"
For her kit-chen late - ly Showed a ta-per's flare".
Ou-vre-moi ta por - te Pour l'a-mour de Dieu!"
Car dans sa cui-si - ne On bat le bri - quet."

After last verse — *Fine*

3. While the rays illumine
Onward Lubin hies.
Quick the dark-eyed woman
At his knocking cries:
"Who is calling? Say thee!"
And he answers low:
"Draw thy latch I pray thee,
Ere the love-moon go".

4. By the moonlight weak'ning
Little meets their sight.
Now the pen they're seeking,
Now they search for light.
What their searching won them
May be less or more,
But I know that on them
Slowly closed the door.

3. *Au clair de la lune,*
L'aimable Lubin
Frappe chez la brune
Ell' répond soudain:
"Qui frapp' de la sorte?"
Il dit à son tour:
"Ouvre-moi ta porte
Pour le Dieu d'amour".

4. *Au clair de la lune,*
On n'y voit qu'un peu
On cherche la plume,
On cherche du feu.
En cherchant d'la sorte
Je n'sais c'qu'on trouva:
Mais j'sais que la porte
Sur eux se ferma.

Cradle Song
Wiegenlied

The collections of folksongs by Brahms, published in 1894, contain no number more appealing than this *Cradle Song.* It has appeared in many translations, not all, it must be said, of equal merit, and the Brahms accompaniment has sometimes been modified. In the version here given effort has been made to adhere closely to the German text, and the accompaniment is authentic.

English version by
WILL EARHART

JOHANNES BRAHMS

Original key - Eb
M.W.& Sons 19438-56

I Love Thee

Ich Liebe Dich

This song was published in 1803, one year before publication of the composer's Eroica Symphony. It bore the title *Zärtliche Liebe* (Tender Love), but has been published in English under the title *Mutual Love*. As Beethoven used the text it begins with the second stanza of Herrosen's poem, *Ich liebe dich*.

A mood rarely captured by any composer other than Beethoven here finds expression. Sincerity and depth of feeling are blended with exquisite purity and simplicity. A sustained tone-line and clear diction that holds no trace of the declamatory are necessary to a right revealment of the nobility and beauty of the song.

English version by
WILL EARHART

L. van BEETHOVEN

I love but thee as thou dost me, At eve as on the
Ich lie - be dich, so wie du mich, am A - bend und am

mor - - row, And ne'er a day has dawned for us But
Mor - - gen, noch war kein Tag, wo du und ich nicht

cresc.

we have shared our— sor - row.
teil - ten uns' - re— Sor - gen.

So—
Auch

dim.

mf

p

Original key - G

M.W.& Sons 19438- 56

Request
Bitte

Of the many songs by Franz, which aggregate only a score fewer than three hundred, the brief song *Bitte* is one of the most admired. Nevertheless it offers few vocal or interpretive difficulties to the student, although it does demand, similarly to all of this composer's songs, depth and truth of understanding. Penetration of the poet's mood is the first step toward such understanding, for from such effort to recreate in himself the individual feeling of the poet did Franz himself approach the composition of his songs.

Text by
NICOLAUS LENAU
English version by
WILL EARHART

ROBERT FRANZ, Op. 9, No. 3

Original key - D♭

M.W. & Sons 19438-56

With the ma-gic of thy dark-ness Take this
Nimm mit dei-nem Zau-ber -dun-kel die -se

world from me a-way, And, en-fold-ing
Welt von hin -nen mir, dass du ü -ber

all my be-ing, Dwell with me for e'er and aye.
mei-nem Le -ben ein -sam schwe-best für und für.

If Thou Be Near

Bist du bei mir

In the notebook for Anna Magdalena Bach for the year 1725 this aria appears as a melody, with a text of unknown authorship, and with only an unfigured bass by way of accompaniment. The mood of the aria, definite as it is in a musical sense, is almost beyond description in words. Serene contemplation, an exaltation that has risen above all worldliness, are apparent. Not a religious song, but one of conjugal affection, it nevertheless interprets human relations in spiritual terms.

English version by
WILL EARHART

J. S. BACH

Andante *(Moderately)*

If thou be near, go I with glad - ness
Bist du bei mir, geh' ich mit Freu - den

to Death and to e - ter - nal Peace, to Death and to e - ter - nal
zum Ster - ben und zu mei - ner Ruh', zum Ster - ben und zu mei - ner

Peace. If thou be near, go I with glad - ness
Ruh'! Bist du bei mir, geh' ich mit Freu - den

Original key—Eb

* This trill and a similar one occurring near the end of the song may be omitted without injury to the interpretation.

**In the first edition this song appeared in A major for low voice. It has been changed to the present key as being more practicable.

M.W.& Sons 19438-56

were thus my end - ing, if thy_ dear hands were laid up - on_ me, and_
wär' so mein En - de, es drück - ten_ dei - ne lie - ben_ Hän - de mir__

gen - tly closed my faith-ful eyes. If thou be_ near, go I with glad - ness
die ge - treu - en Au - gen zu! Bist du_ bei_ mir, geh' ich mit Freu - den

to Death and to e - ter - nal Peace, to _____ Death' and to e - ter - nal Peace.
zum Ster - ben und zu mei - ner Ruh', zum _____ Ster - ben' und zu mei - ner Ruh'!

To The Beloved

An die Geliebte

Beethoven made two settings of this poem. The second, composed possibly in 1812 but not published until 1840, is the one here used. Beethoven's songs, as indeed all his music, are weighted with a deeper emotional tone than the songs of Haydn and Mozart, but the possibility of concentrating a wide glimpse of life into the small limits of an art-song, as Schubert did it, had not yet been revealed. Breadth of expression and care for purely musical values must accordingly be preserved in singing his songs.

English version by
WILL EARHART

L. van BEETHOVEN

Original key - D

M.W. & Sons 19438-56

The Song Of The Drummer

La Chanson du Tambourineur

Crisp in rhythm, precise in tempo, infectiously gay in melody, realistic in text, this song represents the salient characteristics of many French folksongs. But French nicety and lightness of touch are also reflected in the song, and any transgression by the singer in the direction of heavy pleasantry is consequently likely to spoil its charm.

English version by
WILL EARHART

OLD FRENCH SONG
XVIII Century
Accompaniment by
WILL EARHART

1. Oh bring to me my flute now, la tzimm, la tzimm, la tzimm, la la, Oh bring to me my flute now, la tzimm, la tzimm, la
2. For to the war I'm go - ing, la tzimm, la tzimm, la tzimm, la la, For to the war I'm go - ing, la tzimm, la tzimm, la
3. If more he'd pay his sol - diers, la tzimm, la tzimm, la tzimm, la la, If more he'd pay his sol - diers, la tzimm, la tzimm, la

1. *Qu'on m'ap - por - te ma flû - te, la tzimm, la tzimm, la tzimm, la la, Qu'on m'ap - por - te ma flû - te, la tzimm, la tzimm, la*
2. *Pour al - ler à la guer - re, la tzimm, la tzimm, la tzimm, la la, Pour al - ler à la guer - re, la tzimm, la tzimm, la*
3. *S'il pay - ait mieux ses dril - les, la tzimm, la tzimm, la tzimm, la la, S'il pay - ait mieux ses dril - les, la tzimm, la tzimm, la*

la_____ My roll-ing drum as well.
la_____ To serve my king, Loo-ee.
la_____ They'd serve him bet - ter far.   bold.
la_____ *Mon tam-bour-in aus-si.*
la_____ *Ser - vir le roi Lou-is.*
la_____ *Il se - rait mieux ser - vi.*   *- si.*

4	4
O then he'd capture cities,	*Il gagnerait des villes,*
la tzimm, la tzimm, la tzimm, la la,	*la tzimm, la tzimm, la tzimm, la la,*
O then he'd capture cities,	*Il gagnerait des villes,*
la tzimm, la tzimm, la la,	*la tzimm, la tzimm, la la,*
And castles big as well.	*Et des châteaux aussi.*

5	5
He'd marry off his daughters,	*Il marierait ses filles,*
la tzimm, la tzimm, la tzimm, la la,	*la tzimm, la tzimm, la tzimm, la la,*
He'd marry off his daughters,	*Il marierait ses filles,*
la tzimm, la tzimm, la la,	*la tzimm, la tzimm, la la,*
In bargain-matches rare.	*A de fort bons partis.*

6	6
Long live my valiant captain,	*Vive mon capitaine,*
la tzimm, la tzimm, la tzimm, la la,	*la tzimm, la tzimm, la tzimm, la la,*
Long live my valiant captain,	*Vive mon capitaine,*
la tzimm, la tzimm, la la,	*la tzimm, la tzimm, la la,*
And my lieutenant bold.	*Mon lieutenant aussi.*

M.W. & Sons 19438 - 66

Leave Me In Sorrow

Lascia ch'io pianga from "Rinaldo"

Handel's opera Rinaldo, composed in 1711 in two weeks' time, was a notable work in a day when opera had first become a popular form of entertainment. As all such contemporary works, it has long passed from the stage, but remains in memory because of the rare beauty of the excerpt here given. Handel himself showed favor for this melody, for it first appears as a saraband in an opera that he composed seven years earlier. The stately tread of the saraband seems yet to control and give dignity to the passionate musings now reflected in the aria. The original recitative was for soprano and alto. The one here given, of unknown origin, was that used by the celebrated Henrietta Sontag (1804-1854).

English version by
WILL EARHART

G. F. HANDEL

Original key - F

* The Recitative may be omitted, if desired

M.W. & Sons 19438-56

Poco meno lento

O tears as - suag-ing pain's bit - ter rag-ing, From my great tor - ment in
Il duo-lo in-fran-ga que-ste ri - tor-te Dei miei mar - ti - ri, sol

pi - ty free_ me. From my great tor - ment, O set_ me free!
per pie - tà,____ Dei miei mar-ti - ri, sol per_ pie - tà.

Tempo primo

Leave me in sor - row that knows no mor - row; Deep is my_
La - scia ch'io pian-ga mia cru - da sor - te, E che so -

The Cradles
Les Berceaux

Fauré's compositions in larger forms are not as widely current in America as in his native France, but many of his songs are favorably known here. *The Cradles* is one of a score of these that might further enrich the American repertory. It reveals the composer's power to create a distinctive mood or atmosphere, and discloses also his clearly defined melodic originality. The influence of the text upon the music is extremely powerful, leading at times to an almost point to point correspondence; but a sustained melodic sweep is nevertheless a salient feature of the composition to which the singer will need to pay due regard.

SULLY PRUDHOMME
English version by
WILL EARHART

GABRIEL FAURÉ

Original key - c minor

M.W. & Sons 19438-56

dream - ing, un - mind - ful of cra - - dles small,
pren - nent pas gar - - de aux ber - ceaux,

poco rall.   *a tempo*

Rocked by hands of wom - en a - pray - - ing.
Que la main des fem - mes ba - lan - ce.

poco rall.   *a tempo*

p cresc. poco a poco sin' al mf

Soon must come the day of fare - well,
Mais vien - dra le jour des a - dieux,

pp cresc. poco a poco sin' al mf

The vessels tall,
Yet in that day / Et ce jour là les grands vaisseaux,
Flying from port that fades away, / Fuyant le port qui diminue
Feel their great frames held 'neath the sway / Sentent leur masse retenue
Of / Par

Ne'er Shade So Dear

Ombra mai fu

Recitative and Aria, from "Xerxes"

Serse, or *Xerxes*, one of the latest operas Handel composed before turning to the composition of oratorios, was performed early in 1738. The term *Largo*, meaning broad, and holding usually an implication of slow and dignified movement, would almost appear to name a characteristic of much of Handel's music. It has become the title by which this piece, heard now in all sorts of arrangements for instruments and voices, is popularly known. Little but controlled and stately music-making, undisturbed by dramatic pungencies, is needed for bringing about a satisfying performance of the *Aria*.

English version by
WILL EARHART

G. F. HANDEL

Boughs so del - i - cate and ten - der of my
Fron - di te - ne - re e bel - le del mio

tree well be - lov - ed, for you___ is splen - dor wait - ing.
pla - ta - no_a - ma - to, per voi___ ri - splen - de_il fa - to;

Thun - der, light - ning, nor the tem - pest ev - er - more shall dis -
tuo - ni, lam - pi e pro - cel - le non v'ol - trag - gi - no

Original key - F
* The Recitative may be omitted, if desired.

M.W.& Sons 19438-56

turb your peace-ful calm-ness; nor, steal-ing to pro-fane you,
mai la ca-ra pa-ce, nè giun-ga a pro-fa-nar-vi

energico   Largo *(Slowly)*

come spoil-er greed-y.
Au-stro ra-pa-ce!

near, Fair - - est_ mine eyes have seen. Ne'er_ shade so_ dear,
più, ca- -ra ed a - ma - bi - le, om - bra mai_ fu

Made of such ten - der green; Fair - est mine eyes have seen,
di ve - ge - ta - bi - le, ca - ra ed a - ma - bi - le,

To_ heav - en near, To_ heav - en_ near.
so - a - ve più, so - a - ve_ più.

March Of The Kings

La Marche des Rois

(Provençal Noël)

In his music to "L'Arlésienne", Bizet wrought upon this traditional melody with a passion and loveliness that have carried it into the hearts of thousands. But although the music thus gained new gleams and meanings, no treatment could add to the primal strength of the old Noël. The lines of its melody are firm as the everlasting hills, its narrative text glows with fervor. Unconscious dignity and power rest upon it. The singer does not need to labor to make it imposing. Some declamation is called for, it is true, but over emphasis should be avoided. The style is that of a throng in a religious processional, not that of a military march.

English version by
WILL EARHART

Old Provençal Melody
Accompaniment by
WILL EARHART

1. Once at dawn_ I met the brave ar - ray__ Of three great kings up-on a jour-ney
2. Flags in air,_ A sight be-yond com-pare,_ Were play-ing bold-ly with the flaunt-ing

1. De ma - tin_ Ai res-coun-tra lou trin_ De tres grand Rei qu'a-na-voun en vou-
2. Lei drap - eou_Qu'er-oun se-gur fort beou_ Ei ven - tou - let ser-vien de ba - di-

hast - ing; Once at dawn__ I met the brave ar - ray__ Of three great
breez - es; Cam - els fair__ With loads of treas-ure rare,__ Up - on their

ia - gi, De ma - tin__ Ai res-coun-tra lou trin__ De tres grand
na - gi; Lei ca - meou__ Qu'er-oun se - gur fort beou__ Pour-ta - voun

M.W.& Sons 19488-56

3

Wrought in gold
A chariot onward rolled,
And there I saw the kings as meek as angels;
Wrought in gold
A chariot onward rolled,
And o'er it banners waved in manya fold.
The oboe sweet,
In music meet,
The praises high of my Lord was ever sounding.
The oboe sweet,
In music meet,
The glories of my Lord did oft repeat.

3

Dins un char
Daura de touto part,
Vesias lei Rei moudeste coumo d'angi,
Dins un char
Daura de touto part,
Vesias briha de riches estendard;
Ausias d'aubois,
De bellei vois
Que de moun Diou publicavoun lei louangi;
Ausias d'aubois,
De bellei vois
Que disien d'er d'un admirable chois.

4

'Neath the spell
Of tones that pleased me well,
I drew aside to see the chariots gliding;
'Neath the spell
Of sights that pleased me well,
I followed far to see what more befell.
In radiance mild
A lone star smiled,
And shone above, on their way the Magi guiding;
In radiance mild
A lone star smiled,
And gleamed at last above the new-born Child.

4

Esbahi
D'entendre aco d'aqui,
Me siou rangea per veire l'equipagi;
Esbahi
De veire aco d'aqui,
De luen en luen leis ai toujour segui;
L'astre brihant
Qu'ero davan,
Servie de guido, en menant lei tres Rei Magi;
L'astre brihant
Qu'ero davan,
S'arreste net quaut fougue vers l'Enfant.

5

By the stall
In awe the Magi fall,
On bended knee to offer prayers adoring;
By the stall
In awe the Magi fall,
Before the Babe, the new-born Lord of all.
Then Gaspard led
With gold, and said:
"My Lord 'tis Thou art the only King of Glory";
Then Gaspard led
With gold, and said:
"He conquers death; afar the tidings spread".

5

Soun intra
E se soun prousterna,
A douei ginoux, li disien sei priero,
Soun intra
E se soun prousterna,
Davant lou Rei, qu'es nouvelament na:
Gaspard d'abord
Presento l'or
Et dis: Moun Diou, sias lou soulet Rei de gloiro,
Gaspard d'abord
Presento l'or
E dis pertout que ven cassa la Mort.

6

"Incense fine",
Saith Melchior, is Thine;
The hosts of God are 'neath Thy banner standing.
"Incense fine",
Saith Melchior, is Thine,
For Thou in one art King and God divine.
That poor Thou art,
And meek of heart,
Is token rare of the love Thy heart commanding;
That poor Thou art,
And meek of heart,
From Thy divinity can take no part.

6

Per present
Melchior oufre l'encen,
En li disent: Sias lou Diou deis armado;
Per present
Melchior oufre l'encen,
Disent: Sias Rei et sias Diou tout ensen
La paoureta,
L'umilita
De vousto amour soun lei provo assegurado;
La paoureta,
L'umilita
N'empachoun pas vouesto Divinité.

7

"As for me,
I weep, dear Lord, for Thee,
As in my grief this bitter myrrh I proffer;
As for me
I weep, dear Lord, for Thee".
Thus spake Balthazar, faint with agony.
"One day for us,
Upon the cross,
As mortal, Thou for all mortal sin must suffer;
One day for us,
Upon the cross,
Thy death shall purge us all of mortal dross".

7

Quant a ieou
N'en plouri, moun bouen Diou!
En sangloutant vous presenti la mirro;
Quant a ieou
N'en plouri, moun bouen Diou.
Li dis Balthasurd, pu mouart que viou;
Un jour, per nous
Sus uno crous,
Coumo mourtaou fenires nouesti miseri;
Un jour, per nous
Sur uno crous,
Deves mourri per lou salut de tous!

8

Now we sing
In worship of the King,
Baptized by John, in sacred water kneeling;
Now we sing
In worship of the King
Whose law triumphant doth salvation bring.
At solemn board
The water poured He changed to wine,
Then as now His pow'r revealing;
At solemn board
The water poured
He changed to wine; O praise our mighty Lord!

8

Au-jour-d'uei
Es adoura dei Rei,
E bateja dei man de jan Batisto;
Au-jour-d'uei
Es adoura dei Rei
Tout l'univers se soumete a sa lei
Dins un festin
Rende l'aigo en vin:
Aqueou miracle es segur ben de requisto;
Dins un festin
Rende l'aigo en vin:
Nous manifesto soun poude divin.